Shhhh...
A Book About Hearing

by Dana Meachen Rau

illustrated by Rick Peterson

Thanks to our advisers for their expertise, research, and advice:

Angela Busch, M.D., All About Children Pediatrics
Minneapolis, Minnesota

Susan Kesselring, M.A., Literacy Educator
Rosemount-Apple Valley-Eagan (Minnesota) School District

PICTURE WINDOW BOOKS
Minneapolis, Minnesota

Managing Editor: Catherine Neitge
Creative Director: Terri Foley
Art Director: Keith Griffin
Editor: Christianne Jones
Designer: Nathan Gassman
Page production: Picture Window Books
The illustrations in this book are gouache paintings.

Picture Window Books
151 Good Counsel Drive
P.O. Box 669
Mankato, MN 56002-0669
877-845-8392
www.capstonepub.com

Printed in China. 042010 005766

Library of Congress Cataloging-in-Publication Data
Rau, Dana Meachen, 1971-
Shhhh...: a book about hearing / Dana Meachen Rau;
illustrated by Rick Peterson.
p. cm. — (Amazing body)
Includes bibliographical references and index.
ISBN 978-1-4048-1018-1 (hardcover)
ISBN 978-1-4048-6541-9 (saddle-stitched)
1. Hearing—Juvenile literature. 2. Ear—Juvenile
literature. I. Peterson, Rick. II. Title. III. Series.

QP462.2.R38 2005
612.8'5—dc22   2004019168

Thump,
thump,
thump.

What is that sound?

It's a basketball! Every time the ball hits the ground, it makes a thumping sound.

4

When the ball bounces, it sends sounds into the air. Your ear catches these sounds. Hearing is one of your five senses.

Sound moves along wavy paths called sound waves. Your earflap catches the sound waves as they travel past your ears.

6

Many animals have earflaps, too. Elephants have big floppy ones. Cats have triangle-shaped ones.

You hear the sound of the ball when the sound waves enter your ears.

Your earflap sends the sound waves into your ear canal.

The ear canal is a tube that runs from your earflap into your head.

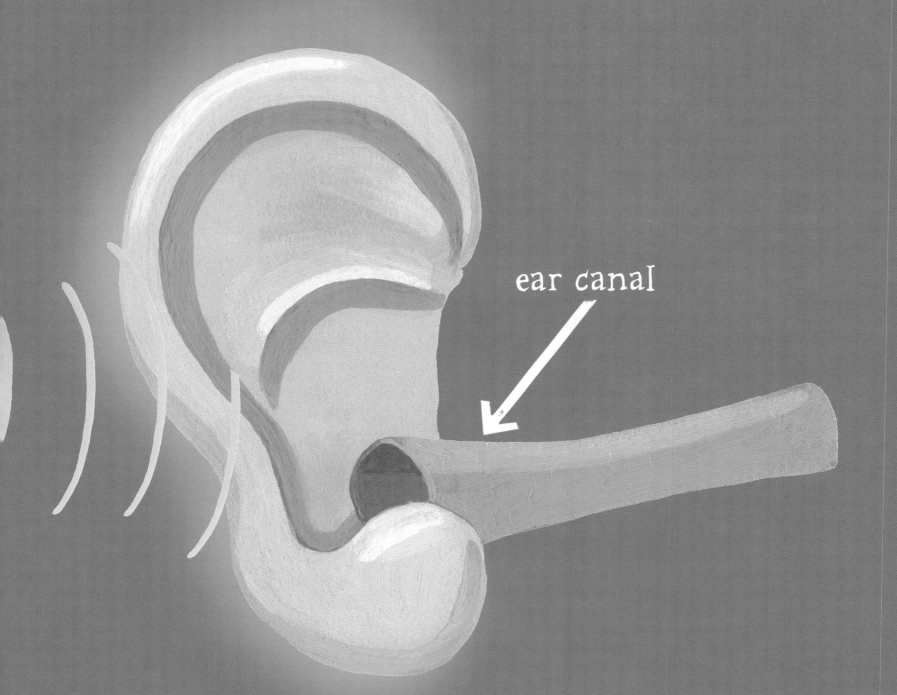

ear canal

At the end of your ear
canal, the sound waves
hit your eardrum.

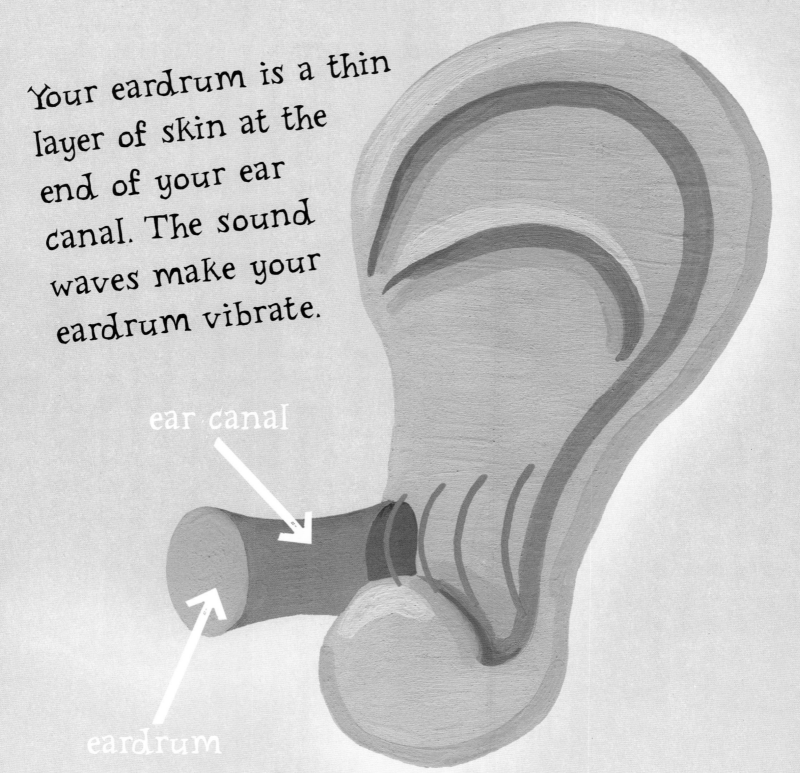

Your eardrum is a thin layer of skin at the end of your ear canal. The sound waves make your eardrum vibrate.

ear canal

eardrum

Your eardrum is connected to the hammer, anvil, and stirrup. When the eardrum vibrates, it shakes the hammer. The hammer shakes the anvil. The anvil shakes the stirrup.

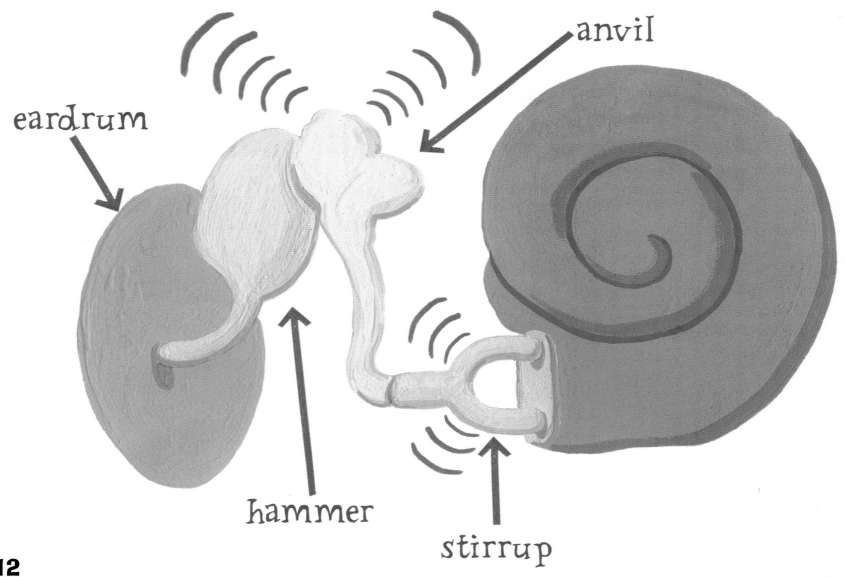

anvil

eardrum

hammer

stirrup

The hammer, anvil, and stirrup are the smallest bones in your body.

The stirrup is attached to the cochlea. The cochlea looks like a seashell. It is filled with liquid.

Shake, shake, shake.

The stirrup shakes against the cochlea. The shaking makes the liquid in the cochlea shake, too.

Tiny hairs inside the cochlea are attached to nerves.

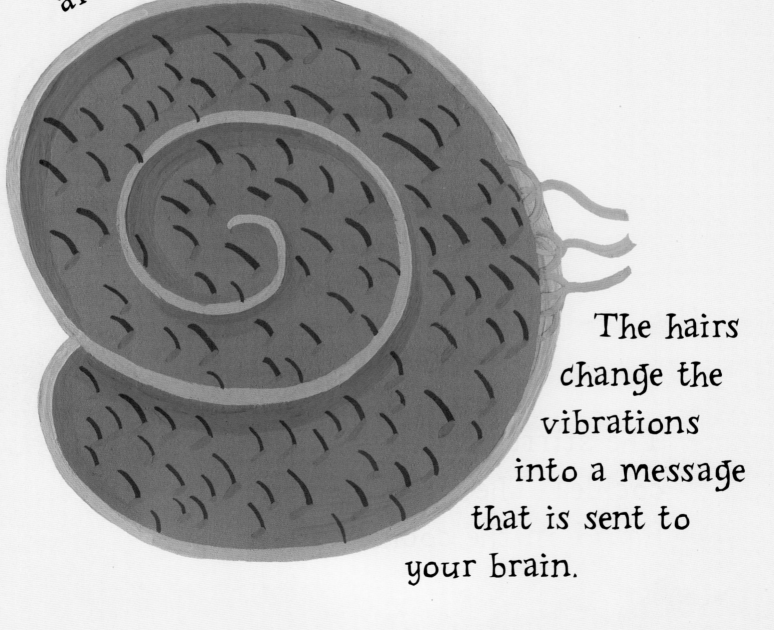

The hairs change the vibrations into a message that is sent to your brain.

Your nerves relay many different types of sound to your brain. Your brain knows the difference between soft, loud, close, or far away sounds.

Your nerves bring the message to the part of your brain in charge of your senses.

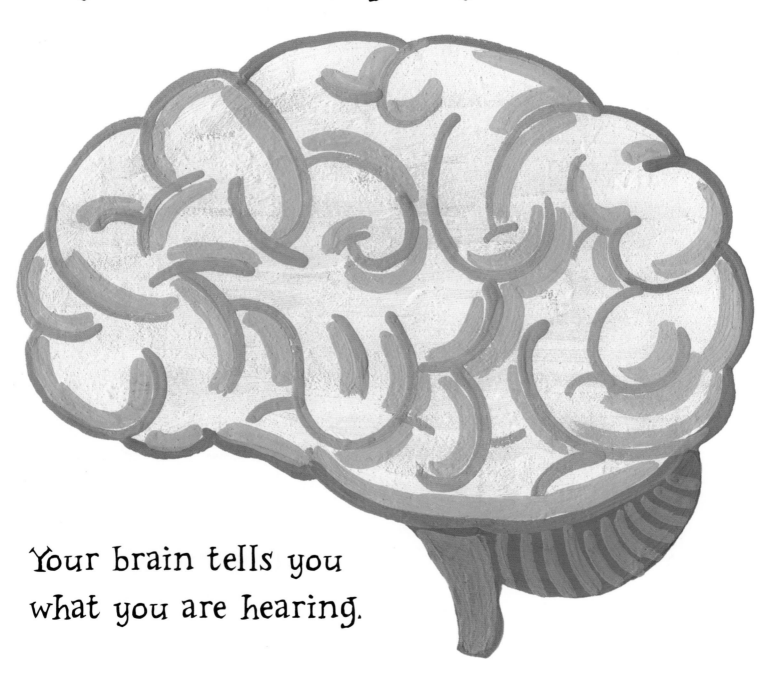

Your brain tells you what you are hearing.

A whisper is a very quiet sound. You have to listen closely to hear it. Cupping your hand around your ear makes it easier for your ear to catch sound waves.

Listen. Do you hear that?

Your brain remembers sounds. When you talk on the phone with a friend, your brain knows who it is. Your brain remembers the sound of your friend's voice.

Thump, thump, thump.

There's that bouncing again. Your ears are always working.

Ear Diagram

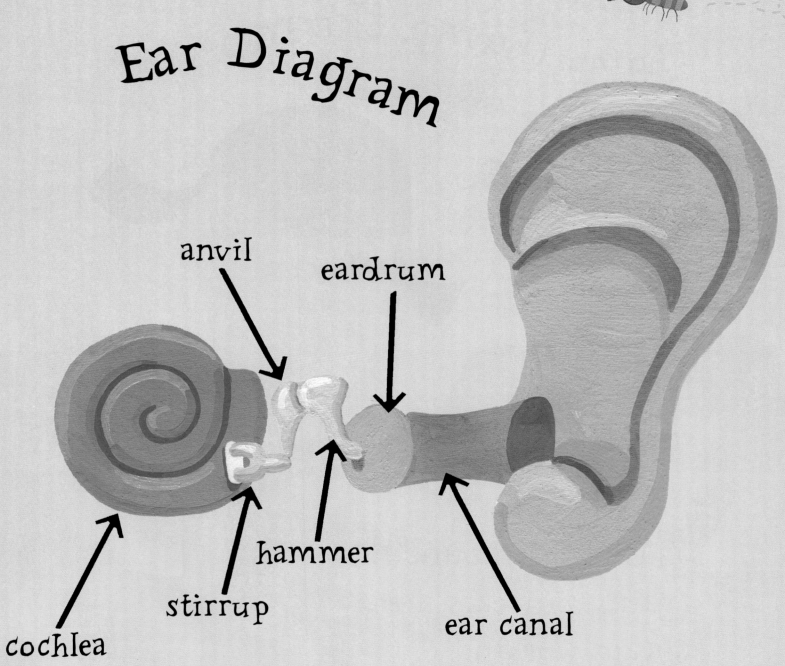

anvil

eardrum

cochlea

stirrup

hammer

ear canal

Fun Facts

- You use your ears for more than just hearing. Some of the parts inside your ears help you keep your balance.

- Some sounds are very high. People can't always hear them. Bats can hear a lot of high sounds that people can't.

- Sticky orange earwax found in your ear canal catches dust and dirt so they don't damage your eardrum.

- Some people get ear infections. This happens when germs get behind your eardrum.

Glossary

cochlea—an organ filled with liquid in the inner ear

ear canal—the tube from your earflap to your middle ear

eardrum—a thin layer of skin at the end of your ear canal

earflap—the part of the ear outside your head

nerves—cords running through your body that get and give messages to your brain

sound wave—the path sound follows as it travels through the air

vibrate—to shake back and forth very quickly

To Learn More

At the Library

Arnold, Caroline. *Did You Hear That? Animals with Super Hearing.* Watertown, Mass.: Charlesbridge, 2001.

Cole, Joanna. *You Can't Smell a Flower with Your Ear! All About your Five Senses.* New York: Grosset & Dunlap, 1994.

Nelson, Robin. *Hearing.* Minneapolis: Lerner Publications, 2002.

On the Web

FactHound offers a safe, fun way to find Web sites related to this book. All of the sites on FactHound have been researched by our staff.

1. Visit www.facthound.com

2. Type in this special code: 1404810188

3. Click on the FETCH IT button.

Your trusty FactHound will fetch the best sites for you!

Index

Look for all of the books in the Amazing Body series:

Bend and Stretch: Learning About Your Bones and Muscles

Breathe In, Breathe Out: Learning About Your Lungs

Gurgles and Growls: Learning About Your Stomach

Look! A Book About Sight

Look, Listen, Taste, Touch, and Smell: Learning About Your Five Senses

Shhhh... A Book About Hearing

Sniff, Sniff: A Book About Smell

Soft and Smooth, Rough and Bumpy: A Book About Touch

Think, Think, Think: Learning About Your Brain

Thump-Thump: Learning About Your Heart

Yum! A Book About Taste